JESUS & THE LAW

Dr. J.C. Matthews

J.C. MATTHEWS ENTERPRISES

DR. J.C. MATTHEWS
JESUS
&
THE LAW
PART OF THE KINGDOM TEACHING SERIES
JURISPRUDENCE
MATTHEW 24:14

Dr. J.C. Matthews

Jesus & The Law

J.C. Matthews Enterprises

Jesus & The Law

ISBN –9798583241729

J.C. Matthews Enterprises LLC, a,k.a. J.C. Matthews Ministries
2931 Ridge Rd
Rockwall, Texas 75032
For more information about J.C. Matthews Ministries. and its products call 1-888-800-4896 or visit www.jcmatthews.org.

Table of Contents

CHAPTER I

Jesus, Legalism & God's Law

One of the greatest obstacles we face in gaining a proper understanding of God's Law in the life of the New Testament church and Jesus' perspective of it, is found in the fact that there are numerous kinds and layers of laws, rules, regulations, commandments and traditions that we have grouped together and refer to as *law*. Some of these laws are issued by civil authorities, while others are the creation of various religious commandments and traditions that were passed down by the elders and religious leadership of the day. Other references to law in the New Testament refer to the very Covenant Law of God and those given to Israel by Moses for the orderly government of God's people within the Covenant Community of faith. In other places, the Jewish people as a whole is referred to as the law, along with the whole of the Old Testament, in particularly the books of Psalms, Deuteronomy and the prophets. With such a wide range of meaning, it is obvious that the context in which the word *law* is used becomes determinative of which law is being referenced.

This is Not That

In the gospel of Mark, we witness Jesus confronting the religious leader on their application and abuse of various man-made laws that where in fact contrary to the very law of God that they claim to be representatives and stewards of. For in Mark chapter 7 we find them questioning Jesus as to why His disciples did not abide by the laws and traditions of the elders. Jesus rebukes them by pointing out that these man-made laws, commandments and traditions, are not God's law, but instead serve to undermine it. Specifically, we read:

"Then the Pharisees and some of the scribes came together to Him, having come from Jerusalem.
2 Now when they saw some of His disciples eat bread with defiled, that is, with unwashed hands, they found fault. 3 For the Pharisees and all the Jews do not eat unless they wash their hands in a special way, holding the ***tradition of the elders.*** *4 When they come from the marketplace, they do not eat unless they wash. And there are many other things which they have received and hold, like the washing of cups, pitchers, copper vessels, and couches.5 Then the Pharisees and scribes asked Him, "Why do Your disciples not walk according to the* ***tradition of the elders****, but eat bread with unwashed hands"?*
6 He answered and said to them, "Well did Isaiah prophesy of you hypocrites, as it is written: 'This people honors Me with their lips, But their heart is far from Me. 7 And in vain they worship Me, Teaching as doctrines the ***commandments of men.****'8 For laying aside t****he commandment of God****, you hold* ***the tradition of men****—the washing of pitchers and cups, and many other such things you do."9 He said to them, "All too well you* ***reject the commandment of God****, that you may keep* ***your tradition****. 10 For Moses said, 'Honor your father and your mother'; and, 'He who curses father or mother, let him be put to death.' 11 But you say, 'If a man says to his father or mother, "Whatever profit you might have*

received from me is Corban"—' (that is, a gift to God), 12 then you no longer let him do anything for his father or his mother, 13 making ***the word of God of no effect*** *through* ***your tradition*** *which you have handed down. And many such things you do" (Mark 7:1-12, NKJV).*

Jesus make it clear that the commandments and traditions of men, were not God's law, but worked to make God's law of no effect! In other words, what they were enforcing as law, was not the Law of God. *This is not that!* Jesus distinguishes the authorship of the law being imposed by the Scribes and Pharisees as being *"your"* traditions, not God's Law!

These commandments and traditions of the elders formed a rigid system of rules that regulated every sphere of life in very fine detail. They covered everything from how far one could walk on the Sabbath, to whether or not you could light a fire after a given time of day. They had grown to be a massive body of case law, where rules were created when a perceived violation of God's Law occurred. Over time these rules and commandments became onerous and a yoke to the people. These extrapolations of the law were originally created by the religious leadership in an effort to prevent people from accidentally breaking the law. They were guardrails to keep one on the path and from straying. However, as the number of these regulations grew and became more granular, they became divorced from its God's spirit and His original intent for giving His law and became a man-made web of religious bondage. As a result of these man-made laws having become divorced from the spiritual aspects of God's Law, one was often forced to break the God's Laws in order to comply with their regulations. These laws, traditions, commandments, rules and regulations included ,and were in addition to, the recognized 613 Laws of Moses. For the 613 Laws of Moses were topical, and covered such things as: Honoring God and His Law (The Torah), Prayer and Blessings, Loving One Another, Caring for the Poor and Unfortunate, Just treatment of strangers, Marriage, Divorce and Family Relationships, Prohibitions and Proper Sexual Immorality, Honoring the Sabbath, Dietary Laws, Business Practices, Servants and Slave relationships, The Making of Vows and Oaths, Jubilee, The Administration of Law and Justice in the Forming of Court and Judicial Procedures, Injury and Damages, Property Rights, Criminal Law, Punishment and Restitution, as well as, Prophecy, Care and Treatment of Animals and Agriculture, Clothing, the Firstborn, The 613 Laws also included regulations for the Priesthood, Tithes and Offerings, The Temple and Sacrifices, Ritual Purity, including Lepers and Leprosy, concluding with instructions for the King, Nazarites and the proper Conducting of War. In examining the 613 Laws of Moses, none of them regulated or related to the washing of hands, bowls or cups before eating. These were added as further regulations of the people's lives that served as a yoke upon them. As a matter of fact, these additional man-made laws were specifically prohibited by God in several places in scripture. Specifically, we find the people of Israel being warned in Deuteronomy 4:

> *"You shall not add to the word which I command you, nor take from it, that you may keep the commandments of the Lord your God which I command you" (Deuteronomy 4:2, NKJV) (See also Deuteronomy 12:32).*

The Pharisees and scribes where not only breaking God's law through adding to it, but they were also breaking it by their failure to observe it themselves. In Matthew 23,

Jesus again confronts the Scribes and Pharisees pointing out that they were not law keepers, but legalist, law breakers and hypocrites. Specifically, Jesus said:

> *"The scribes and the Pharisees sit in Moses' seat. [3] Therefore whatever they tell you to observe, that observe and do, <u>but do not do according to their works; for they say, and do not do</u>. [4] For they bind heavy burdens, hard to bear, and lay them on men's shoulders; but they themselves will not move them with one of their fingers. [5] But all their works they do to be seen by men. ... [13] "But woe to you, scribes and Pharisees, <u>hypocrites</u>! For you shut up the kingdom of heaven against men; for you neither go in yourselves, nor do you allow those who are entering to go in. [14] Woe to you, scribes and Pharisees, <u>hypocrites</u>! For you devour widows' houses, and for a pretense make long prayers. Therefore you will receive greater condemnation.' ...[15] "Woe to you, scribes and Pharisees, <u>hypocrites</u>! For you travel land and sea to win one proselyte, and when he is won, you make him twice as much a son of hell as yourselves.' ... [23] "Woe to you, scribes and Pharisees, <u>hypocrites</u>! For you pay tithe of mint and anise and cummin, and have neglected the weightier matters of the law: justice and mercy and faith. These you ought to have done, without leaving the others undone. [24] Blind guides, who strain out a gnat and swallow a camel! [25] "Woe to*

> *you, scribes and Pharisees, hypocrites! For you cleanse the outside of the cup and dish, but inside they are full of extortion and self-indulgence. [26] Blind Pharisee, first cleanse the inside of the cup and dish, that the outside of them may be clean also. [27] "Woe to you, scribes and Pharisees, hypocrites! For you are like whitewashed tombs which indeed appear beautiful outwardly, but inside are full of dead men's bones and all uncleanness. [28] Even so you also outwardly appear righteous to men, but inside you are full of hypocrisy and lawlessness" (Matthew 23:1-5a,13-15, 23-28, NKJV)(Underline added).*

Jesus calls them *hypocrites* and *lawless*! They were teaching the people one thing, while doing another. Many within the church today call those who espouse the view that we are to abide by God's law *Pharisees*. This is due to the perception that they were law keepers, but in truth they were law breakers and legalist. Jesus advises the people to honor the Scribes and Pharisees position as rulers, but at the same time warned them not to follow their example due to the fact that they themselves were violators of the God's law. They enforced the letter devoid of love and the spirit in which God gave His Law for the purpose of controlling the people and the praise of men It is clear from the text that Jesus views God's law as being in force and relevant, but not in the manner in which it was being taught and administered by the religious leadership! The fact that the law being administered by the Pharisees is described as being a *"heavy burden"* is evidence that what was being taught was not God's Law or Commandments. For scripture plainly states that God's *"commandments are **not burdensome**"* (1John 5:3b, NKJV). It was the man-made law, abuse and perversion of God's Law that caused men to groan under the weight of these regulations imposed upon them by the religious leadership. Similar sentiment is found in the New Testament concerning these man-made *commandments. laws, traditions and regulations* created by men. Specifically, we read:

- **Titus 1:13b-16 (NKJV)** - *"Therefore rebuke them sharply, that they may be sound in the faith, 14 not giving heed to Jewish fables and commandments of men who turn from the truth. 15 Unto the pure all things are pure: but unto them that are defiled and unbelieving is nothing pure; but even their mind and conscience is defiled. 16 They profess that they know God; but in works they deny him, being abominable, and disobedient, and unto every good work reprobate."*

- **Colossians 2:20-23 (NKJV)** – *"Therefore, if you died with Christ from the basic principles of the world, why, as though living in the world, do you subject yourselves to regulations - 21 "Do not touch, do not taste, do not handle," 22 which all concern things which perish with the using—according to the commandments and doctrines of men? 23 These things indeed have an appearance of wisdom in self-imposed religion, false humility, and neglect of the body, but are of no value against the indulgence of the flesh"*
- **1Peter 1:18-19 (NKJV)** - *"knowing that you were not redeemed with corruptible things, like silver or gold, from your aimless conduct received by tradition from your fathers, 19 but with the precious blood of Christ, as of a lamb without blemish and without spot"*
- **Galatians 4:8-9 KJV** - *"Howbeit then, when ye knew not God, ye did service unto them which by nature are no gods. 9 But now, after that ye have known God, or rather are known of God, how turn ye again to the weak and beggarly elements, whereunto ye desire again to be in bondage?"*

Jesus, Paul and Peter, all in their writings, describe these commandments, laws, traditions and regulations as being fables and self-imposed religious requirements that are of no value against carnality, but work to turn men away from God and into further bondage.

In contrast, God's law does not produce bondage, but liberty in the life of His people. We experience freedom from sin's dominion over our lives, providing a guiding principle by which we live and enjoy the protections given us in God's Law. God's law is not a burden when used within, and for, its intended purpose. The Apostle Paul confirmed this when he wrote: *"we know that the law is good, if a man use it lawfully" (1Timothy 1:8).* What had become a burden upon the people was a perverted form and use of the law; it having become separated from its original purpose. This is the definition of *perversion*, it being the practicing of a thing separated from its purpose, which generally produces problems, not peace. Problems are inherent in our practicing something devoid of its purpose, because those who promote the purposeless practice replace the original purpose with their own. This is what the scribes and Pharisees did with God's law. By continuing to refer to their religious practices as God's Law, they were able to borrow from its authority in order to legitimize their personal agendas exercising power over the people without question. This is in essence legalism practiced by legalist. Legalism, within the context of scripture, is not the act of *keeping God's law*, but the religious *misuse* of it for personal and illegitimate ends.

As we can see from the above, there were various kinds of law within the religious community that were being espoused as God's law, but were in fact man made rules and regulations that placed a yoke upon the people. These laws were outgrowths of God's Covenant Law and the 613 Laws given by Moses for the maintenance of order, justice and well-being within the Covenant Community of God. In addition to these additional laws and interpretations by the religious leadership, we find within the New Testament context the abuse of God's law, in that it was imposed upon the people as a means of justification with God. These Judaizers were teaching and requiring Gentiles to be circumcised and keep the law in order for them saved. This is where we find the apostle Paul apologetic writings in his defense of the foundations of our justification found in God's grace and the work of Jesus Christ on our behalf. The problem with all of these abuses is found in the fact that they originate with God's Law, but are perversions of it employed for personal and illegitimate ends. These legalists were not law keepers, but violators of God's Law and in many cases enemies of the cross, in that their doctrines placed men's faith in their obedience for justification, instead of in Christ. We must keep this in mind when reading Paul and his repudiation of law, and pay attention to the context in which he is speaking. For if you were to pay close attention to the text that most rely upon in rejecting the law within the New Testament church, you will notice that the words justification, for righteousness sake or righteousness is mentioned. This is an indication that Paul is specifically addressing an abuse of the Law, and not rejecting God's Law as being relevant and proper within the New Testament church!

Jesus, as well as Paul, during their ministries sought to clarity and distinguish God's law from the abuse and misuse perpetrated by the existing religious establishment. In other words, *this* which has become a burden upon the peoples through it legalist enforcement, is not *that* which God gave His people for their instruction, guidance prosperity and protection. *This is not that!* Unfortunately, many within the church today have not taken the time or effort to do the same, and have concluded that Jesus came to do away with God's Law and that Paul teaches that it should be set aside due to it being contrary to the revelation of God's grace and the work of Christ accomplished on our behalf. We will see in our study of Jesus' relationship to God's Law that He infect did not come to destroy it, but instead, to resurrect it from the graveyard of religion and restore it within the Covenant Community of God to its original purpose and former glory.

CHAPTER II

Jesus & God's Law

It may come as a surprise to many that the longest recorded and most significant messages recorded by Jesus in the Gospels does not concern the issues of salvation or even heaven, but God's Kingdom and His Law. This message is often referred to as the *Sermon on the Mount* and comprises a full 3 chapters of Matthew's gospel. Specifically, we see Jesus, as an initial matter, address the establishment of the culture of His Kingdom on earth, while providing in-depth teaching on the revelation and restoration of God's Law within it! It may come as an even greater surprise, in light of the perception that Jesus, in one form or another, undid or replaced the Law, that He in this discourse reveals Himself as the *Original Law Giver!* However, before we examine this revelation in greater detail, I want to turn our attention to statements made by Jesus that confirm that: (1) He in fact did not come to do away with the Law, but to build upon, clarify, restore and even expand it, and (2) He saw Himself as the Author and giver of the Law, while also being the summation of it.

To begin, let us take a look at contents of His famous Sermon on the Mount where He highlights the two major objectives of His earthly ministry, i.e. the Kingdom and God's Law. Jesus begins by placing His teaching within its proper context of His Kingdom. Specifically, He begins his instruction by pronouncing several blessings, also known as the Beatitudes, when He said:

> *"Blessed are the poor in spirit: for theirs is the kingdom of heaven. **4** Blessed are they that mourn: for they shall be comforted. **5** Blessed are the meek:*

> *for they shall inherit the earth.* ***6*** *Blessed are they which do hunger and thirst after righteousness: for they shall be filled.* ***7*** *Blessed are the merciful: for they shall obtain mercy.* ***8*** *Blessed are the pure in heart: for they shall see God.* ***9*** *Blessed are the peacemakers: for they shall be called the children of God.* ***10*** *Blessed are they which are persecuted for righteousness' sake: for theirs is the kingdom of heaven.* ***11*** *Blessed are ye, when men shall revile you, and persecute you, and shall say all manner of evil against you falsely, for my sake." (Matthew 5:3-11, NKJV).*

Notice, that when Jesus speaks of the *Kingdom*, He does so in the *present tense*, using the word "is" as opposed to the verb *"shall"*. He is communicating to the people that the long-awaited Kingdom that they have been seeking over the centuries is here or *in their midst*. From verses 12 thru 16 He goes on to teach the importance of good works in the life of the people. This is in stark contrast to much of the teaching today that denounces *works* as being necessary under the New Covenant. This is in large part due to the church's Salvation Paradigm approach to scripture and its interpretation of *works* being a means by which man strives to merit God's blessings and promises. The Apostle Paul makes this same distinction of works for righteousness sake and works a necessary and preordained part of the believer's life, when he wrote:

> *"For it is by free grace (God's unmerited favor) that you are saved (delivered from judgment and made partakers of Christ's salvation) through [your] faith. And this [salvation] is not of yourselves [of your own doing, it came not through your own striving], but it is the gift of God;* ***9*** *Not because of works [not the fulfillment of the Law's demands], lest any man should boast. [It is not the result of what anyone can possibly do, so no one can pride himself in it or take glory to himself.]* ***10*** *For we are God's [own] handiwork (His workmanship), [recreated in Christ Jesus, [born anew] that we may do those good works which God predestined (planned beforehand) for us [taking paths which He prepared ahead of time], that we should walk in them [living the good life which He prearranged and made ready for us to live]." (Ephesians 2:8-10, AMPC).*

Paul makes it clear that works are not a means by which we earn or merit right standing with God or His blessings, but that they are received through grace and faith. However, he goest on to point out that those who have been recreated in Christ, or born again, were recreated or predestined to do good works as sons of God! From a Kingdom Paradigm perspective, or relating to those who are already saved, works are the evidence that we present to the world that we have indeed been transformed and children of God. Beginning at verse 17, Jesus begin the process of revealing and restoring the spiritual substance of God's law in contrast to the external code of conduct developed and implemented by the religious leaders of the day. He begins by addressing the misconception that His coming was for the purpose of nullifying the Law of God. It was as if the Holy Spirit knew that men would assert that this would be His purpose. Jesus dismisses this presumption by authoritatively declaring:

> *"Think not that I am come to destroy the law, or the prophets: I am not come to destroy, but to fulfil.*
> ***18*** *For verily I say unto you, Till heaven and earth pass, one jot or one tittle shall in no wise pass from the law, till all be fulfilled.* ***19*** *Whosoever therefore shall break one of these least commandments, and shall teach men so, he shall be called the least in the kingdom of heaven: but whosoever shall do and teach them, the same shall be called great in the kingdom of heaven" (Matthew 5:17-19, NKJV).*

Wow! Not only does Jesus emphatically reject the idea that He came to destroy the Law, but that those who teach others to set it aside would be considered the *least* in the Kingdom! Again, Jesus had not gone to the cross yet and is speaking of the Old Testament Law given by God. Many who hold to the perspective that Jesus' statement concerning *fulfilling the law*, is somehow a reference to Him bringing it to an end. This is quickly dismissed by taking a look at the word translated "*fulfill*" in the text. The word in the text is the Greek word "*pleroo*", which can be translated to mean to: *complete, end, fill or accomplish*. However, it also is understood to mean: *to verify, to make full or to fully preach*. With these seemingly contradictory meanings assigned to the same word, we must look to the prophet Isaiah's statement concerning why Jesus came for clarification on the issue. For in Isaiah chapter 42:21, we read:

> "*The LORD is well pleased for his righteousness' sake; he will magnify the law and make it honourable*" (KJV).

The word "*magnify*" in the text is the Hebrew word "*gadal*", which means to cause to: *make large and excellent*. The word *honorable* is the Hebrew word "*adar*", which literally means to *expand or make glorious*. Based on the above, Isaiah's understanding of what Jesus' relationship to the Law was not to diminish or shrink it in any fashion, but to *enlarge, expand and restore its to its former glory!* This is what we see Christ doing in His teaching where He does not simply confine adultery to the *act* of sleeping with another's spouse, but expands it to include the wrong thoughts harbored in one's heart for another's spouse. Similarly, we see the same thing with His teaching on murder. He does not confined murder to the *act* of taking of another's life, but speaks of the root of murder, which is anger from which the act ultimately precedes. In verse 20, Jesus points out that this external code of conduct by which one has traditionally and religiously been held accountable is insufficient in the Kingdom. He specifically, calls this out by saying:

> *"For I say unto you, That except your righteousness shall exceed the righteousness of the scribes and Pharisees, ye shall in no case enter into the kingdom of heaven."*

It is clear from the text that Jesus was not *rolling back* the law or teaching that it is to be set aside, but as Isaiah pointed out, He is *expanding* our understanding of it to exceed the external righteousness required by the scribes and Pharisees. In essences, Jesus was resurrecting the Law from the graveyard of its *current carnal* understanding, and restoring it to is former internal and spiritual glory and work, which God intended from the very beginning.

Christ the Law Giver

In an effort to gain even greater insight into Christ's relationship to God's Law, we must take an even closer look at His teaching on the Mount. Specifically, we read in Matthew 5:

> *"Do not think that I came to destroy the Law or the Prophets. I did not come to destroy but to fulfill.*
> *18 For assuredly, I say to you, till heaven and earth pass away, one jot or one tittle will by no means pass from the law till all is*
> *fulfilled. 19 Whoever therefore breaks one of the least of these commandments, and teaches men so, shall be called least in the kingdom of heaven; but whoever does and teaches them, he shall be called*
> *great in the kingdom of heaven. 20* ***For I say*** *to you, that unless your righteousness exceeds the righteousness of the scribes and Pharisees, you will*
> *by no means enter the kingdom of heaven.21* ***"You have heard*** *that it was said to those of old, 'You shall not murder, and whoever murders will be in*
> *danger of the judgment.' 22* ***But I say*** *to you that whoever is angry with his brother without a*

cause\shall be in danger of the judgment. And whoever says to his brother, 'Raca!' shall be in danger of the council. But whoever says, 'You fool!' shall be in danger of hell fire. 23 *Therefore if you bring your gift to the altar, and there remember that your brother has something against you,* 24 *leave your gift there before the altar, and go your way. First be reconciled to your brother, and then come and offer your gift.* 25 *Agree with your adversary quickly, while you are on the way with him, lest your adversary deliver you to the judge, the judge hand you over to the officer, and you be thrown into prison.* 26 *Assuredly, I say to you, you will by no means get out of there till you have paid the last penny.* 27 *"**You have heard** that it was said to those of old, 'You shall not commit adultery.'* 28 ***But I say** to you that whoever looks at a woman to lust for her has already committed adultery with her in his heart.* 29 *If your right eye causes you to sin, pluck it out and cast it from you; for it is more profitable for you that one of your members perish, than for your whole body to be cast into hell.* 30 *And if your right hand causes you to sin, cut it off and cast it from you; for it is more profitable for you that one of your members perish, than for your whole body to be cast into hell.* 31 *"Furthermore* **it has been said,** *Whoever divorces his wife, let him give her a certificate of divorce.'* 32 ***But I say** to you that whoever divorces his wife for any reason except sexual immorality*

causes her to commit adultery; and whoever
marries a woman who is divorced commits
adultery.[33] "Again ***you have heard*** *that it was*
said to those of old, 'You shall not swear falsely,
but shall perform your oaths to the Lord.' [34] ***But I***
say *to you, do not swear at all: neither by heaven,*
for it is God's throne; [35] nor by the earth, for it is His
footstool; nor by Jerusalem, for it is the city of the
great King. [36] Nor shall you swear by your head,
because you cannot make one hair white or
black. [37] But let your 'Yes' be 'Yes,' and your 'No,'
'No.' For whatever is more than these is from the
evil one. [38] ***"You have heard*** *that it was said, 'An*
eye for an eye and a tooth for a tooth.' [39] ***But I tell***
you *not to resist an evil person. But whoever slaps*
you on your right cheek, turn the other to him
also. [40] If anyone wants to sue you and take away
your tunic, let him have your cloak also. [41] And
whoever compels you to go one mile, go with him
two. [42] Give to him who asks you, and from him
who wants to borrow from you do not turn
away.[43] ***"You have heard*** *that it was said, 'You*
shall love your neighbor and hate your
enemy.' [44] ***But I say*** *to you, love your enemies, bless*
those who curse you, do good to those who hate you,
and pray for those who spitefully use you and
persecute you, [45] that you may be sons of your
Father in heaven; for He makes His sun rise on the
evil and on the good, and sends rain on the just and
on the unjust" (Matthew 5:17-45, NKJV).

One must wonder, how is it that Jesus could take such liberty in adding to or expanding God's law in His teachings? Specifically, in statements such as:

- *[21]"**You have heard** that it was said to those of old, 'You shall not murder, and whoever murders will be in danger of the judgment.' **But I say** to you that whoever is angry with his brother without a cause shall be in danger of the judgment.*
- *[27] "**You have heard** that it was said to those of old, 'You shall not commit adultery.' **But I say** to you that whoever looks at a woman to lust for her has already committed adultery with her in his heart.*
- *[31] "Furthermore **it has been said**, 'Whoever divorces his wife, let him give her a certificate of divorce.' **But I say** to you that whoever divorces his wife for any reason except sexual immorality causes her to commit adultery; and whoever marries a woman who is divorced commits adultery.*
- *[33] "Again **you have heard** that it was said to those of old, 'You shall not swear falsely, but shall perform your oaths to the Lord.' **But I say** to you, do not swear at all: neither by heaven, for it is God's throne; nor by the earth, for it is His footstool; nor by Jerusalem, for it is the city of the great King.*

- 38 *"**You have heard** that it was said, 'An eye for an eye and a tooth for a tooth.' **But I tell you** not to resist an evil person. But whoever slaps you on your right cheek, turn the other to him also.*
- 43 *"**You have heard** that it was said, 'You shall love your neighbor and hate your enemy.' **But I say** to you, love your enemies, bless those who curse you, do good to those who hate you, and pray for those who spitefully use you and persecute you, that you may be sons of your Father in heaven; for He makes His sun rise on the evil and on the good, and sends rain on the just and on the unjust"*

Throughout Jesus' teaching we witness him declaring: *"You have heard …"* or *"It has been said …"*. These are direct references to statements found in God's Law and the Laws given to Moses for the governance of God's Covenant people. However, shortly after Jesus these statements we hear Him also declare: *"But I say"* or *"But I tell you …"*. The word *"but"* is significant in that it signals a change in direction, or even a negation, of what was previous said, which were statements concerning God's Law! _This is significant in light of their being a direct prohibition in scripture from God concerning the adding or taking away from God's Law. Specifically, we find recorded in the book of Deuteronomy:

> *"You shall not add to the word which I am commanding you, nor take away from it, that you may keep the commandments of the Lord your God which I command you (Deuteronomy 4:2 (NASB),*

And,

> *"Whatever I command you, you shall be careful to do; you shall not add to nor take away from it. Deuteronomy 12:32 (NASB).*

If Jesus were not the Original Law Giver, He was in violation of this prohibition. In making the statement "But you have heard ...", Jesus was directly making reference to the Commandments and law of God given the people concerning the prohibition against murder, adultery, divorce, swearing, revenge etc ... (See Matthew 5:21-22, 27-28, 31-32, 33-34,38-39, 43-44). Jesus in making these statements reveals Himself as the Original Law Giver in the flesh! For both Isaiah and James agree that: the Lord is our judge and lawgiver ...", for "there is only one Lawgiver and Judge, the one who is able to save and destroy. ..." , who we understand to be none other than our Lord and Savior Jesus the Christ! (See Isaiah 33:22 and James 4:12).

The Author's Authority

There is a legal principle of jurisprudence concerning how laws are changed that provides us great insight into how Jesus could take such liberty to amend or add to God's Law. The legal principle, simply stated, is: *"Only the Author of a law has the authority to add to, amend, change or nullify a law"*. In other words, if Jesus was not the original giver of the law, He was not authorized to add, amend or change it. We see this same principle at work in our legal system today as it relates to the annulling, amending or changing laws that govern our lives at every level. Take for instance, the legislature of Oklahoma. It cannot add to, amend, change or nullify laws passed by the Texas Legislature. Likewise, Canada cannot add to, amend or invalidate any portion of the laws that govern the United States. Similarly, a son or child cannot add to, amend, change or nullify the law established by their father or parent for the household. They don't have the authority to do so. Only the *maker or author* of the law can do so. In like manner, if Jesus was not the *Original Law Giver*, He could not say, as He does in Matthew 5, *"You have heard it said ..., but I say ..."*. Jesus had to be the *Original Law Giver* for Him to add to or expand God's Law in light of a direct prohibition by God recorded in scripture.

It is clear that Jesus did not see His statements as nullifying or contradicting God's Law, but rather as a clarification or expansion of its meaning, thereby revealing the original and spiritual intent of God for His law, while at the same time, distinguishing it from the performance-based system of rules established by the scribes and Pharisees. They had turned God's Law into a Code of Conduct that one was to obey in order to be adjudged righteous. This performance based religious adherence, was not God's intent in giving His law, not to mention the multitude of additional laws and traditions added to it by the religious leaders that in effect caused God's Law to become of no effect (Mark 7:13). Christ willingness to take the liberty of expanding God's Law not only revealed that His purpose was not to *destroy, diminish* or set aside the Law of God, but to also reveal Himself as the *Original Law Giver!*

CHAPTER III

Christophany

In order to assist in our understanding of Christ being the Lawgiver of the Old Testament, we must first explore the reality of the Biblical concepts of *Christophany and Theophany*. It is widely agreed upon in Christian orthodoxy that Christ appeared in various forms throughout the Old Testament and is understood to be God in human form. The Biblical concepts of *Christophany and Theophany* in scripture plays a central role in understanding many of the Old Testament texts in which God is said to be seen or discernible by human beings. For the Bible plainly states that God is *spirit* and that no man has ever seen Him at any time (John 1:18, 1John 4:12). As a matter of fact, it is said that no man can see God and live (Exodus 33:22). As a result, when we come across scripture that declares that a man has seen God, we must look at how it is that God is said to have been seen and consider that this expression of God may very well be His Son - Jesus Christ manifested. Oftentimes when scripture speaks of a *Theophany* it is making reference to a manifestation that has made God discernible to the senses, such as a v*oice, wind, cloud, pillar of fire or a burning bush*. However, when we speak of a *Christophany*, we generally are not speaking of a supernatural manifestation that consists of fire, wind or a voice, but one that is more personal, such as an *angel* or a *human-being*.

Christ's work in this world did not begin in the New Testament, but began at the onset of the world, in that scripture reveals that He is the one who created all things (John 1:1-3, Colossians 1:16). However, when it comes to man, it appears that the Father committed a special role to the Son, especially after the fall. For we told in Genesis

3:8 that Adam and Eve, after the fall:

> *"[H]eard the voice of the Lord God walking in the garden in the cool of the day: and Adam and his wife hid themselves from the presence of the Lord God amongst the trees of the garden."*

One has to wonder, how is it that scripture says that God's "voice" was *walking* in the Garden? It is possible to hear the sound of someone's footsteps, but it could not be said that it was their voice walking. Scripture is specific, in that it was the *"**voice** of the Lord God walking in the garden"*. Some clarity to this phenomenon may be found in the *Targum Onkelos*, which is an Aramaic translation of the Hebrew text, which translates this same verse to say:

> *"And they heard the voice of God as **the Word of the Lord God** walking in the garden in the evening of the day" (bold added).*

The title *"the Word of Lord" and "the Word of God"*, is found throughout the Old and New Testament, while more specifically in the New Testament, it is a reference to Jesus *the Word made flesh*. The Apostle John in his gospel points this out when he wrote:

> *In the beginning was the Word, and the Word was with God, and the Word was God. 2 He was in the beginning with God. 3 All things were made through Him, and without Him nothing was made that was made.' ... He was in the world, and the world was made through Him, and the world did not know Him.' ... 'And the Word became flesh and dwelt among us, and we beheld His glory, the glory as of the only begotten of the Father, full of grace and truth." (John 1:1-3, 10 and 14, NKJV).*

John says that not only was the word with God, but the *"Word was God ..."* This unity is referenced in Genesis 1:26, where God speaks of Himself in the plural, when He declared, *"Let Us make man ...."* (Genesis 1:26). Therefore, it is clear that Jesus was not only the creative Word of God (John 1:1-3, Colossians 1:16), but is considered God Himself! This become important when we read later in scripture that God is said to be seen by men, while scripture plainly states the *no man can see God and live* (See Exodus 33:20). The Apostle John in his epistle goes on to explain that the *Word of God was* manifested as the Son, in the person of Jesus Christ.

Specifically, he wrote:

> *"That which was from the beginning, which we have heard, which we have seen with our eyes, which we have looked upon, and our hands have handled, concerning the Word of life— 2 the life was manifested, and we have seen, and bear witness, and declare to you that eternal life which was with the Father and was manifested to us— 3 that which we have seen and heard we declare to you, that you also may have fellowship with us; and truly our fellowship is with the Father and with His Son Jesus Christ.*

Theologian and preach Jonathan Edwards, in his book entitled: History of the Work of Redemption, noted that it was readily understood amongst the Reformers and puritans that Christ appears throughout the Old Testament as the manifestation of God. Specifically, he wrote:

> *"Therefore, when we read in sacred history what God did from time to time towards his church and people, and what he said to them, and how he revealed himself to them, we are to understand it especially of the second person of the Trinity. When we read of God's appearing after the fall, from time to time, in some visible form or outward symbol of his presence, we are ordinarily, if not universally, to understand it especially of the second person of*

> *the Trinity' ... 'He is therefore called "the image of the invisible God," Col. i.15.; intimating, that though God the Father be invisible, yet Christ is his image or presentation, by which he is seen, or by which the church of God hath often had a representation of him, that is not invisible▪ and in particular that Christ has after appeared in an human form". (History of the Work of Redemption, Jonathan Edwards, p.20-21)*

Therefore, when it is said that Jacob wrestled with God, it is understood that it was in fact Christ the Son with whom he contended. Specifically, we read in Genesis 32:

> *"Then Jacob was left alone; and a **Man** wrestled with him until the breaking of day. 25 Now when He saw that He did not prevail against him, He touched the socket of his hip; and the socket of Jacob's hip was out of joint as He wrestled with him.' 26 ... 28 'And He said, "Your name shall no longer be called Jacob, but Israel; for you have struggled with **God** and with men, and have prevailed."... 30 'So Jacob called the name of the place Peniel: "For I have **seen God** face to face, and my life is preserved." (Genesis 32:24-25, 28, 30, NKJV, bold added).*

In the above text, it is clear that Jacob wrestled with what he understood to be a *Man*. Jacob understood that the Man he wrestled was God in human form. The word

"Man" in the text is capitalized to indicate that this was not just any man. This Man was *God in the flesh,* who Jacob declared he saw *face to face,* and yet lived. In other places in the Old Testament, we are presented with similar Christophanies that takes the form of an angel, specifically *the Angel of the Lord,* which is later called *the Son of God.* We read in the book of Daniel where an *angel* appears and is understood to be a *man*, which King Nebuchadnezzar later describes as being *the Son of God.* Specifically, in Daniel 3, we hear King Nebuchadnezzar inquiring about the three Hebrew boys that were thrown into the fiery furnace, asking:

> *"Did not we cast three men bound into the midst of the fire? They answered and said unto he king, True, O king. He answered and said, Lo, I see four men loose, walking in the midst of the fire, and they have no hurt; and the form of the fourth is like* ***the Son of God****"* (Daniel 3:24-25, KJV, *bold added*).

He goes on in verse 28 to say:

> *Blessed be the God of Shadrach, Meshach, and Abednego, who hath sent* ***his angel****, and delivered his servants that trusted in him" (Daniel 3:28 (KJV, bold added)*

It is clear from the above text that the person in the fire, which he first describes as *"the Son of God"*, he also refers to as *God's "angel"*. This definite article *"the"* combined with the capitalization of the *"S"* in the word *"Son"*, distinguishes the One in the fire from being any other *angel or son of God,* but *"the Angel of the Lord"* and *"the Son of God"* - Jesus Christ!

Jesus - The Angel of the Lord

Throughout the Old Testament we are introduced to one called the "The Angel of the Lord". Many struggle with the revelation of Jesus being the *Angel of the Lord* due to our having come to confine our understanding of an *angel* to being a wholly *spiritual being.* However, the word *angel*, as it is rendered in the Hebrew, simply means "*messenger*". The word translated "angel" in the Old Testament is the Hebrew word ***"malak"*** (H4397), which carries the meaning: *to be dispatched as a deputy; or a messenger, specifically of God, that is an angel, (also a prophet, priest, teacher, ambassador or king) ...".* Therefore, the title *"the Angel of the Lord"* also carries the meaning of being one who is designated as a *prophet,* *priest, teacher, ambassador and/or king* sent by God and not simply a spirit being. In light of the aforementioned, we can understand the *Angel of the Lord* as being a *special messenger sent by God!*

In addition, we find a similar reference to *the Angel of the Lord* in the book of Judges where we read:

> *"And **the Angel of the Lord** appeared to the woman and said to her, "Indeed now, you are barren and have borne no children, but you shall conceive and bear a son. Now therefore, please be careful not to drink wine or similar drink, and not to eat anything unclean. For behold, you shall conceive and bear a son. And no razor shall come upon his head, for the child shall be a Nazirite to God from the womb; and he shall begin to deliver Israel out of the hand of the Philistines. "So the woman came and told her husband, saying, "A **Man of God** came to me, and His countenance was like the countenance of the **Angel of God,** very awesome; but I did not ask Him where He was from, and He did not tell me His name. And He said to me, 'Behold, you shall conceive and bear a son. Now drink no wine or similar drink, nor eat anything unclean, for the child shall be a Nazirite to God from the womb to the day of his death.' "Then Manoah*

> *prayed to the Lord, and said, "O my Lord, please let the **Man of God** whom You sent come to us again and teach us what we shall do for the child who will be born." And God listened to the voice of Manoah, and the **Angel of God** came to the woman again as she was sitting in the field; but Manoah her husband was not with her. Then the woman ran in haste and told her husband, and said to him, "Look, **the Man** who came to me the other day has just now appeared to me!" So Manoah arose and followed his wife. When he came to **the Man**, he said to Him, "Are You the Man who spoke to this woman?" And He said, "I am."* (Judges 13:3-11, NKJV. Bold and underline added).

Again, Monoah, Sampson mother, describes *"the Angel of the Lord"* as being the *"Man of God"*. As we saw in Genesis, when Jacob wrestled with the Man, who is later referred to as God, the word *"Man"* is capitalized by the writer to communicate that this was no mere human being. Again, the word *"the"*, being placed before the word Man, is a definite article used to specify and distinguish Him from other men. Just as King Nebuchadnezzar in Daniel 3 identified the one in the fire as *"the Son of God"*, Monoah does the same thing to distinguish *"the Man"* she met from any other human being. I addition, it is evident from the text that_Monoah knew she was speaking to a *human being* for she, like Abraham, entreated her visitor to *eat a meal* with her (Judges 6:15, Genesis 18:1-5). This only make sense if she understood that the one before her was a physical being needing nourishment for his body, or was a human. Further evidence that she perceived t*he Angel of the Lord* to be a *human being* is found in her describing Him as having a *"countenance"*, or a *"face"* that could be seen. In other words, she is attempting to describe a human figure with a naturally discernible face that is endowed with glory. This could be likened to the face of Moses as it glew with glory, after spending time in the very presence of God when he came down from the Mount (Exodus 34:29-30). Similarly, we see Gideon speaking of *the Angel of the Lord* and perceives Him to be a human being, for he too prepares a meal for Him to eat, while considering himself to have spoken with God face to face. For scripture reveals that after having spoken with the Angel of the Lord, that:

> *"And Gideon went in, and made ready a kid, and unleavened cakes of an ephah of flour: the flesh he put in a basket, and he put the broth in a pot, and brought it out unto him under the oak, and*

> *presented it. 20 And the **angle of God** said unto him, Take the flesh and the unleavened cakes, and lay them upon this rock, and pour out the broth. And he did so. 21 Then the **angel of the Lord** put forth the end of the staff that was in his hand, and touched the flesh and the unleavened cakes; and there rose up fire out of the rock, and consumed the flesh and the unleavened cakes. Then the **angel of the Lord** departed out of his sight. 22 And when Gideon perceived that he was an **angel of the Lord,** Gideon said, Alas, O Lord God! for because I have seen an **angel of the Lord** face to face" (Judges 6:19-22, KJV, bold added).*

It is clear that Gideon perceived the angel he spoke to as being more than a mere messenger, by him referring to the Angel as being the "*Lord God*" Himself. Earlier in the book of Judges, the Angel of the LORD reveals to Gideon that He was the one who brought Israel out of Egypt. Specifically, we read:

> *"**The angel of the LORD** went up from Gilgal to Bokim and said to the Israelites, "<u>I brought you out of Egypt</u> into this land that I swore to give your ancestors, and I said I would never break my covenant with you." (Judges 2:1, NLT, bold added).*

Furthermore, in the New Testament, the apostle Jude reveals in his epistle, that the One called *the Angel of the Lord* that delivered the people from bondage was, in fact, Jesus ***Himself***. Specifically, he wrote:

> *"Although you are fully aware of this, I want to remind you that after* ***Jesus*** *had delivered His people* ***out of the land of Egypt,*** *He destroyed those who did not believe." (*Jude 1:5, Berean Study Bible).

The apostle Paul confirms Jude's conclusion that Christ Himself delivered Israel from bondage and accompanied them in the wilderness, when he wrote to the church at Corinth explaining:

> *"Moreover, brethren, I would not that ye should be ignorant, how that all our fathers were under the cloud, and all passed through the sea; 2 And were all baptized unto Moses in the cloud and in the sea; 3 And did all eat the same spiritual meat; 4 And did all drink the same spiritual drink: for they drank of that spiritual Rock that followed them: and that Rock* ***was Christ."*** *... 'Neither let us commit fornication, as some of them committed, and fell in one day three and twenty thousand. 9 Neither let us* ***tempt Christ,*** *as some of them also tempted, and were destroyed of serpents.1Corinthians 10:1-4, 8-9 (KJV, bold added).*

Based on the above texts, it is safe to conclude that *the Angel of the Lord* and *Jesus* are one in the same'. If we were to examine scripture further, we would discover that not only was the *Angel of the Lord* responsible for delivering Israel from Egypt and accompanied them, while being tested through their journey in the wilderness, but that He was also the One who is said to have given the Law to Moses. Specifically, in the book of Acts we are told that:

> *"This is that Moses who said to the children of Israel, 'The Lord your God will raise up for you a Prophet like me from your brethren. Him you shall hear.'* ***38*** *"This is he who was in the congregation in the wilderness with* ***the Angel*** *who spoke to him on Mount Sinai, and with our fathers, the one who received the living oracles to give to us, ..."* (Acts 7:37-38, KJV).

It is clear from the above texts that scripture identifies Jesus our Lord, as being *the Angel of the Lord,* who: (1) was tested in the wilderness, (2) recognized as God, and the (3) gave Moses the Covenant Law on Mount Sinai!

It is interesting to note that Jude said that the first church was *fully aware* of this and understood that Christ was the *Deliverer* of Israel from Egypt! (See Jude 1:5), and therefore the Angel responsible for giving the Law of God, as confirmed in Acts 7:53, which states: *"you who have received the law that was given through angels but have not obeyed it" (NIV).* The Apostles, James, Jude and Paul are not the only ones in New Testament who recognize Jesus as being present in the Old Testament in the form of a Man, Angel or more specifically - *God*, for Jesus Himself plainly said so. When speaking to the Jews, Jesus revealed Himself as being the great *"I AM"*, which identified Himself as being the God who spoke to Moses. Specifically, Jesus said:

> *"Your father Abraham rejoiced to see My day, and he saw it and was glad." Then the Jews said to Him, "You are not yet fifty years old, and have You seen Abraham?" Jesus said to them, "Most assuredly, I say to you, before Abraham was, I AM"* (John 8:56-58, NKJV).

The people clearly understood what Jesus meant by stating that He was the *"I AM"* that existed before Abraham, for they took up stone to stone Him for blasphemy.

By examining Scripture, we discover that Christ's purpose for coming was not to bring an *end* to the Law, but that He in fact was the return of the *Law Giver* Himself, sent to expand, magnify and return the law to its former glory and honor. Just as Jesus Himself stated, *I did not come to destroy the Law*, but to fulfill the righteousness of it. For it is true that Christ is the end of the law <u>*for righteousness*</u> sake to everyone who believes (Romans 10:4), while at the same time, He by no means came to put an end to God's Law! For He is the Original Law Giver!

Grace, Truth and the Law

Many struggle today with the idea of Christ being the Law Giver of Sinai, for they have been taught to believe that He was the *end* of the law, and replaced the original Covenant Law of God. This is primarily based on their misperception of Law and its purpose. They perceive the Old Testament Law and God's grace as being contrary to one another, which is a fruit of the church's Salvation Paradigm perspective and approach to scripture. Many point to the first chapter of John's gospel as support of this position, where we read: *"For the law was given through Moses, but grace and truth came through Jesus Christ" (John 1:17, KJV).* It is important to pay attention to the text itself, for the word *"but"* is *italicized,* indicating that it is not found in the original text, but was later added by the translators. The vast majority of the contemporary translation, translate this same text, to read: *"For the Law was given through Moses; grace and truth were realized through Jesus Christ."* When read as originally written, we see that the Law, as given by Moses, is not negated or in apposition to, the grace and truth realized in Christ Jesus. Furthermore, when we read the context and surrounding verses of the text we discover that the law given by Moses is seen as a provision of grace that was followed up by the realization or manifestation of this grace in Jesus Christ. If we were to include verse 16 with 17, without the erroneous injection of the word *but* we discover that the Law is seen as a grace, that was followed up by more grace, which was found in the person and revelation of Jesus Christ.

Specifically, in the New International Version (NIV) translation, we read: *"Out of his fullness we have all received* ***grace*** *in place of* ***grace*** *already given. For the* *law was given through Moses; grace and truth came through Jesus Christ."* If we were to consider the two text together, we discover that the grace that is presently is being received is a reference to the grace and truth found in part be of verse 17, which is the revelation of Jesus Christ, while the grace already received is a reference to part a of verse 17, or the law given by Moses. Taken in this light, we discover that the law given through Moses and the grace and truth realized in Jesus Christ are in measure different, but in substance the same. For in our study of the law given at Sinai, we discover that God sees the act of giving His law as an act of grace and being the foundation of truth for His people. For in the preparation of giving His people His Law for a second time, we find God declaring His grace and graciousness upon Moses and the people more than 10 times in the space of 10 verses! (See Exodus 33:12-19; 34:6-9). The also Psalmist recognized the Law as being a provision of grace, for he is heard asking God to: *"grant me your law graciously"* (Psalms 119:29b, NKJV).

Therefore, Christ, is the embodiment of the full measure of grace and truth given to men, which was first revealed in substance in the Law of God. For the writer of Hebrews points this out when he wrote of Christ:

> *"Behold, I Have come (in the scroll of the Book it is written of Me) to do your will, of God"* (Hebrews 10:7, NASB).

In light of the above, we see that what was written in the scroll of the book (or the Law) was fully realized the person of Jesus Christ.

CHAPTER IV

Christ's New Commandments

As stated earlier, many today believe that one of the main purposes for Jesus' coming was to do away with the Old Testament Law and replace it with His own law, which they summarize as being the *"Law of Love"*. They believe this in large part due to Jesus' statement to His disciples that He was giving them a *New Commandment*. Specifically, He declared:

> *"A new commandment I give unto you, That ye love one another; as I have loved you, that ye also love one another. By this shall all men know that ye are my disciples, if ye have love one to another" (John 13:34-35, NKJV).*

However, upon closer inspection of this "new law", we discover that it is not new in *substance,* nor a repudiation or replacement of the original Law of God, but is in fact a summation and clarification of the Old. For Jesus Himself said that *"I have kept My Father's commandments" (John 15:10).* This is what the Apostle John meant when he wrote:

> *"Brethren, I write no new commandment to you, but an old commandment which you have had from the beginning. The old commandment is the word which you heard from the beginning" (1John 2:7, NKJV).*

Jesus calls His commandment *new* because He directs us to follow His pattern or to imitate Him in His keeping of God's Law. If we were to look at God's Commandments, we would discover that they are actually two (2) commandments founded in love: Love God and Love one another. This *"new"* commandment was in essence the spirit and substance of the old or original Commandments of God. Jesus did not have to remind the people that they were to love God, which is a summation of the first 4 Commandments, for they already knew and understood this to be a pre-eminent requirement of man. However, Jesus thought it necessary to remind them of the need to unconditionally love one another, as He had done of them, thereby keeping the remaining 6 Commandments of God. Jesus confirmed this understanding of the whole law being found within the *command to love*, when He was asked which is the greatest of God's commandments. To this Jesus replied:

> *"Love the Lord your God with all your heart and with all your soul and with all your mind.' This is the first and greatest commandment. And the second is like it: 'Love your neighbor as yourself.' All the Law and the Prophets hang on these two commandments"* (NIV).

Paul confirms this understanding when he wrote:

> *"[F]or he who loves another has fulfilled the law. For the commandments, "You shall not commit adultery," "You shall not murder," "You shall not steal," "You shall not bear false witness," "You shall not covet," and if there is any other commandment, are <u>all summed up</u> in this saying, namely, "You shall love your neighbor as yourself." Love does no harm to a neighbor; therefore love is the fulfillment of the law" (Romans 13:8b-10, NKJV) (Underline added).*

An easy way to conceptualize God's Ten Commandments as still being wholly contained within the 2

Commandments given by Christ, is by giving you a practical example of how this can be so. Consider this: If each commandment represents **$1.00,** and you to asked me for $10.00, and I gave you **two $5.00** bills, instead of **10 singles**, you still received **$10.00.** Just because it came in the form of two $5 dollar bills does not mean you did not receive **$10.00.** The **$10.00** is wholly found in the two bills you received. Similarly, the 2 Commandments of love Christ gave in Matthew 22:37-40, are in sum and substance the same 10 Commandments given on Mount Sinai! From this perspective, nothing has been lost or set aside, but simply summarized for the Covenant people of God! Similarly, Christ's "New Commandments" to *love* is an expression of all 10 Commandments, i.e. to love God and others as ourselves. Just as Paul explained: *"he who loves another has fulfilled the law" (Romans 13:8b).* By keeping Christ's New Commandments, we fulfill the *whole* of God's Law, in that love is the foundational thread from which all the Commandments are comprised. As a matter of fact, Jesus plainly says this when questioned about God's Commandments. Specifically, we read: Jesus said to him,

> *"You shall love the* L*ORD your God with all your heart, with all your soul, and with all your mind.'* [38] *This is the first and great commandment. And the second is like it: 'You shall love your neighbor as yourself.'* [40] *On these two commandments hang all the Law and the Prophets" (Matthew 22:37-20, NKJV).*

In other words, *love* is the summation and full expression of what was originally given by God to His people in the Old Testament! Therefore, Christ's New Commandment was not a call to set God's original Commandments aside, but to keep them just as He did, by loving God first and foremost, as well as, our fellow man.

The Law to Love

In many respects, the word *love* suffers from the same abuse as the word *law* when it is removed from its proper context and intent. There are things that we do or don't do in the name of *"love"* that are in truth something altogether different. We are told to love people when they engage in conduct that is obviously wrong, and if we tell them that what they are doing is wrong, we are said to be operating outside of love. From this perspective, love has *devolved* to meaning that we must allow people to do whatever they please, whether right or wrong, for fear of being accused of judging them. Just as, it is not love to allow a child to play with fire, it is likewise not love to allow someone to engage in conduct that is harmful to them, both naturally and spiritually.

Similarly, it is so with law. There are many forms and kinds of love that should not be confused with one another. For in the Greek language there are at least 3 major categories of love: *agape, eros and philia. Agape* is considered a familial love that God expresses toward all His creation. It is an unconditional love that transcends the senses and emotions, but if founded in the essence of God. It is a spiritual love that the Bible describes as being a fruit of God's spirit (Galatians 5:22) and the ultimate of His gifts (1Corinthians 13:13). *Philia* is a loving affection that we are to demonstrate to our fellow human beings. It is the bond of respect and proper honor due to our fellow man. It is the loyalty and friendship between equals that enables us to see and esteem one another properly. *Eros*, on the other hand, is an *erotic*, sexual or sensual love that is a product of our passions and emotions. It is the love held between spouses and is not unconditional or founded in loyalty, friendship or honor of the other. Although all of these words are translated *"love"* in the English language they each have very specific meanings that differ widely from one another. The same can be said about the word "law". When speaking of love, it is just as important to know the context and purpose in which the word is being used. It would be a grave mistake to apply the word love (Eros) in a conversation concerning a child. However, it would be perfectly appropriate to use the word *agape.*

Just as it would be inappropriate and an abuse of the word *love* to use it out of its proper context, due to the various kinds and meanings of love, we must resist the temptation of grouping the various kinds of law found in scripture together and calling what is actually the religious laws, commandments and traditions of men - God's Law. When we take the time to distinguish the various kinds of law found in the Bible, we discover that God's Law is truly unique and an expression of His Love toward us, that is neither a burden or curse; *"For this is the love of God, that we keep his commandments: and his commandments are not grievous" (1John 5:3, KJV).*

However, many within the church today characterize God's law as being a curse, death sentence or yoke. Love is not a curse, death nor bondage. Many describe God's Original Law as such because of our seeming inability to conform ourselves to them. However, the same can be said of Christ New Commandment to love one another as He has loved us. The love that Christ is speaking is not a feeling or emotion, but a selfless, giving and forgiving love that is a fruit of God's Holy Spirit. It is not an external act, but an internal reality that must be received and cultivated by the individual in order for them to be able to manifest it in their lives. It is supernatural, in that it is not natural for men to love in this manner, for we are inherently selfish. This is true even within the New Testament church. Therefore, it could not be said that Christ Commandments to love is not for the church simply because it is not something that can be done in the flesh, and that many if not most, who profess to be saved fail to demonstrate. Like the God's Commandments of old, we love not to be loved by God, but because we have already received His love. Love is a fruit of God's covenant, presence and Spirit that empowers us to live godly and selfless lives. Acts or works of love do not make us righteous, but is the fruit or evidence that God is in us, thereby empowering us to manifest the love of God to others.

In summary, if Jesus came to *do away with* the *old* law, then He Himself would not have kept it. The Apostle Paul explains in his letter to the Romans that Christ is the end of the law for "*righteousness sake*" (Romans 10:4), but not an end of the Law, for he goes on to testify that the law is *holy and good* (Romans 7:12). The New Law of Christ to Love is a summarization of the whole law of God, and in no way implies that it is a replacement of the Old, but is an expression of its true purpose and substance.

CHAPTER V

Christ the Commandment Keeper

Jesus not only keep God's Law Himself, but taught it throughout His earthly ministry to be observed. As we look at the text below, we find that Jesus taught all 10 of God's Commandments and in many cases expounding a higher degree of obedience, not a lesser one. Below I have listed the Commandment in order along with their corresponding references found in the New Testament for our consideration.

> **Commandment I** - *"I am the LORD your God, who brought you out of the land of Egypt, out of the house of bondage. You shall have no other gods before Me"*

(Exodus 20:2-3).

- **Matthew 4:10** - You shall worship the LORD your God, and Him only you shall serve".

Commandment II - *"You shall not make for yourself a carved image—any likeness of anything that is in heaven above, or that is in the earth beneath, or that is in the water under the earth; you shall not bow down to them nor serve them" (Exodus 20:4-5).*

- **Matthew 4:10** – "You shall worship the LORD your God, and Him only you shall serve" (Mat 4:10).
- **Luke 4:8** - "You shall worship the LORD your God, and Him only you shall serve"

Commandment III - *"Thou shalt not take the name of the Lord thy God in vain; for the Lord will not hold him guiltless that taketh his name in vain." (Exodus 20:7)*

- **Matthew 12:31** - "Therefore I say to you, every sin and blasphemy will be forgiven men, but the blasphemy against the Spirit will not be forgiven men"

Commandment IV - *"Remember the sabbath day, to keep it holy" (Exodus 20:8).*

- **Mark 2:27** - 'The Sabbath was made for man, and not man for the Sabbath. Therefore, the Son of

Man is also Lord of the Sabbath'".

Commandment V- *"Honour thy father and thy mother: that thy days may be long upon the land which the Lord thy God giveth thee." (Exodus 20:12).*

- **Matthew 15:4** -" For God commanded saying, 'Honor your father and your mother' and 'He who curses father or mother, let him be put to death'"

Commandment VI- *"Thou shalt not kill"* (Exodus 20:13).

- **Matthew 5:21-22** - "You have heard that it was said to those of old, 'You shall not murder', and whoever murders will be in danger of the judgment. But I say to you that whoever is angry with his brother without a cause shall be in danger of the judgment"
- **Luke 18:20** - "You know the commandments...Do not murder"

Commandment VII - *"Thou shalt not commit adultery"* (Exodus 20:14).

- **Matthew 5:27-28** – "You have heard that it was said to those of old, 'You shall not commit adultery'. But I say to you that whoever looks at a woman to lust for her has already committed adultery with her in his heart"

Commandment VIII - *"Thou shalt not steal" (Exodus 20:15).*

- **Mark 10:19** "Do not steal".
- **Luke 18:20** – 'You know the commandments: ... Do not steal".

Commandment IX - *"Thou shalt not bear false witness against thy neighbor"* (Exodus 20:16).

- **Matthew 5:33-34** - "Again you have heard that it was said to those of old, 'You shall not swear falsely, but shall perform your oaths to the Lord. But I say to you, do not swear at all"
- **Mark 10:19 -" Do** not bear false witness"
- **Luke 18:20** - "You know the commandments: ...Do not bear false witness"

Commandment X - "Thou shalt not covet thy neighbor's house, thou shalt not covet thy neighbor's wife, nor his manservant, nor his maidservant, nor his ox, nor his ass, nor any thing that is thy neighbor's" (Exodus 20:17).

- **Mark 7:22-23** – *" ...covetousness...All these evil things come from within and defile a man".*

It is evident from the above that Jesus not only kept God's Commandments, but taught others to do the same. When examining the Commandments themselves, we discover that there is nothing inherent in them that is abrasive to grace or faith. To suggest that the keeping of the Commandments is an impossibility for a spiritually born-again believer, is to suggest that what Christ accomplished for us, in renewing us spiritually, was incomplete. For we find in scripture several instances where spiritually dead men are said to have kept the Commandments or were perfect concerning God's Law. Specifically, we read in the book of Luke 1:

> *"There was in the days of Herod, the king of Judaea, a certain priest named Zacharias, of the course of Abia: and his wife was of the daughters of Aaron, and her name was Elisabeth.And they were both righteous before God, walking in all the commandments and ordinances of the Lord blameless" (Luke 1:5-6, KJV).*

In addition, the Apostle Paul, in speaking of his life before coming to Christ, said:

> *"Though I might also have confidence in the flesh. If any other man thinketh that he hath whereof he might trust in the flesh, I more: Circumcised the eighth day, of the stock of Israel, of the tribe of Benjamin, an Hebrew of the Hebrews; as touching the law, a Pharisee; Concerning zeal, persecuting the church; touching the righteousness which is in the law, blameless" (Philippians 3:4-6).*

The words translated as blameless have the meaning of being without *fault* or *faultless.* It is clear from the above text that the keeping of the Commandments are not outside of the ability of man, as it is taught today. For it would be unjust of God to require something of man that He Himself had not provided him the ability to do. To do so would be to tempt man, and scripture is clear that God tempts no man (James 1:13). Just as the Tree of Knowledge God placed in the Garden was not placed there to test man, but to provide him the opportunity to exercise His free will to honor God as God!

Obedience to God's Commands should be a fruit of our new man, empowered and led by God's Holy Spirit in our desire to honor God and our fellow man. It is only when God's Commandments and Law are forced into, and misused as, a being a means of obtaining righteousness, do we see the friction develop between Law and grace.

About Dr. J.C. Matthews

Dr. J.C. Matthews is an author, pastor, mentor and international speaker who has embraced his assignment of advancing God's Kingdom through understanding, by providing instruction for the Body of Christ concerning the concepts, laws and principles upon which God's Kingdom operates. He has embraced his assignment through the mentoring. Of pastors and leaders, writing of books, conducting workshops and the establishment of the International Kingdom Institute (IKI) and Reign International Ministries, while also functioning as the Apostolic overseer of the International Association of Ambassadors.

J.C. possesses a B.A in Political Science, as well as a Juris Doctorate (J.D.) degree, with an emphasis in Labor and Employment Law. J.C. was twice the recipient of the prestigious *"Who's Who Among American Law Students Award"* in recognition of his outstanding study of law, in addition to being honored by the Ohio State Senate's General Assembly as an Urban All-American. JC's legal training and keen understanding of the Bible enables him to effectively communicate in a practical and simplistic manner seemingly complex concepts, laws and principles of the Kingdom. J.C. and his wife Gena, reside in the Dallas/ Fort Worth, Texas Metroplex.

For more information visit. www.jcmatthews.org.

Printed in Great Britain
by Amazon

28929989R00046